Editor
Karen Tam Froloff

Editor/Consultant
Kiran Prasad Upadhyay

Managing Editor
Karen J. Goldfluss, M.S. Ed.

Editor-in-Chief
Sharon Coan, M.S. Ed.

Illustrator
Agnes S. Palinay

Cover Artist
Leslie Palmer

Art Coordinator
Kevin Barnes

Art Director
CJae Froshay

Imaging
James Edward Grace

Product Manager
Phil Garcia

Publishers
Rachelle Cracchiolo, M.S. Ed.
Mary Dupuy Smith, M.S. Ed.

EXPLORING WORLD BELIEFS
Hinduism

Author

Gabriel Arquilevich

Teacher Created Materials, Inc.
6421 Industry Way
Westminster, CA 92683
www.teachercreated.com
ISBN-0-7439-3681-7
©2002 Teacher Created Materials, Inc.
Made in U.S.A.

Table of Contents

Introduction

Why Teach Religion?

If your students were asked what they know about Hinduism, Islam, Buddhism, Judaism, Sikhs, or Christianity, they might very well respond with a limited amount of information. Although they are impacted almost daily with information related directly or indirectly to religious issues, they often know little about the religions themselves or the lives of the great spiritual leaders.

Why has the study of religion been neglected? In the early 1960s, the Supreme Court declared state-sponsored religious activities within the public schools to be unconstitutional. However, the Court emphasized that learning about religion is essential. Despite the importance of religion in history and culture, most schools have traditionally kept a distance. Fortunately, this distance is being bridged.

As our world becomes more interdependent, there is a need to awaken to one another's spiritual heritage. Throughout history, the world has been shaped by people's religious beliefs. To teach history without religion is equivalent to teaching biology without reference to the human body. School boards across the nation now recognize this issue and have begun to advocate religious studies within the framework of history.

Religious studies foster tolerance. This is, perhaps, the most valuable lesson. Racism and stereotypes are born largely out of ignorance. How wonderful to give students the opportunity to listen to a Buddhist speaker or to visit a synagogue and ask questions of a rabbi. These kinds of direct contacts are invaluable.

Meeting Standards

The National Council for the Social Studies (NCSS) developed curriculum standards in the mid 1990s. These standards have since become widely used in districts and states as they determine essential knowledge and skills acquisition for students. At least two of the ten themes that constitute the social studies framework standards address the study of institutions, cultures, and beliefs. Theme I (Culture), for example, asks students to consider how belief systems, including religion, impact culture. Theme V (Individuals, Groups, and Institutions) challenges students to study the ways in which institutions and religions develop and how they influence (and are influenced by) individuals, groups, and cultures.

Within the NCSS framework, these themes are addressed for all students (early grades through high school). Therefore, support materials such as the books in this series, *Exploring World Beliefs*, are important resources for teachers to use as they work toward meeting standards in the classroom.

Introduction

Religions Originating in South Asia

Share with students the following information:

The Hindu, Buddhist, and Sikh religions originated in the South Asian subcontinent comprising India and Pakistan, beginning with Hinduism as early as 2000 BCE. These three religions differ from the Semitic faiths in some of their most basic beliefs. Hinduism, for example, is a polytheistic religion, meaning that Hindus may believe in various forms of God. (*Poly* means many, while *theism* means belief in God or gods.) Buddhists, on the other hand, do not necessarily believe in God at all. The Sikh religion, the youngest of these faiths, is monotheistic (believing in one God) like the Semitic faiths.

The Indus valley, nurtured by the Indus River, is the birthplace of Hinduism. The Buddha delivered his first sermon at the city of Sarnath near the sacred Hindu city of Benares. To the North is Amritsar, the spiritual center of the Sikh religion. As you can see, this area of the world was the starting point for many religions. Hindus number over 800 million worldwide and make up a large majority of the one billion population of the present day India. There are about 20 million Sikhs with about 80 percent living in India. Buddhism expanded into the rest of Asia to become the dominant faith in China, Japan, and many countries of South East Asia. In India, Buddhists are now a small minority.

About Date References

The abbreviations BCE, BC, AD, and CE are common terms used to reference time. (In this series, BCE and CE are used.) Some students may not be familiar with one or more of these terms. Use page 47 to introduce or review the abbreviations with students.

Suggestions for the Teacher

The books in this series present content that introduces students to several world beliefs. Various terms, phrases, and general content may, at times, be difficult for students to comprehend. It is suggested that segments containing intense factual content be read and discussed together. Have students keep a journal in which they outline important information and maintain a glossary of new terms and their meanings.

The Indus Valley Civilization

Look at the map of the Indus Valley on page 6. This area, now shared largely by Pakistan and a portion by India, is the birthplace of Hinduism. Hinduism is a complex faith with a history that can be traced back five thousand years to the people of the Indus Valley.

Most of what we know of the Indus people comes from archaeological findings. Surveys done with the help of satellites using modern technology such as infrared photography, and artifacts and relics dating back as early as 4000 BCE, tell the story of a civilization flourishing with craftsmanship, agriculture, and religious life. As you will see, many of these early practices and beliefs still shape Hinduism.

One such example is the Indus people's emphasis on cleanliness or ritual bathing. Mohenjo Daro, one of the major Indus cities, contained a huge water tank for public bathing. Old and famous Hindu temples are usually found in the places where water is naturally available.

Another lasting legacy of Hinduism is found in the abundance of terra-cotta figurines unearthed in the Indus Valley. Popular among these small ceramic statuettes were depictions of women. Among them is the Mother Goddess, which has many forms in the Hindu faith and thus plays many roles. She is viewed as the ultimate source of strength and as a symbol of fertility. The concepts of rebirth and continuity that the Mother Goddess represents are still very important to the Hindu religion. According to the teachings of Hinduism, when a person dies, it is only the body that dies while the Atma, the soul, is immortal.

Ceramic seals also tell us something about the Indus' religious beliefs. Among the most common designs is that of the bull. The bull is the means of transport of Lord Shiva, one of the most revered Hindu gods.

The inhabitants of the Indus Valley were an agricultural people, growing crops and raising animals. Living on the banks of the Indus River, dependent on its nourishment and renewal, there was a deep reverence for water. Water still remains sacred to Hindus.

Comprehension Questions

1. How did researchers discover most of the information about the Indus people?

   _____

2. List two findings and briefly explain their links to Hinduism.

   _____

   _____

   _____

3. How did the Indus people survive? How does it relate to their religious worship?

   _____

   _____

   _____

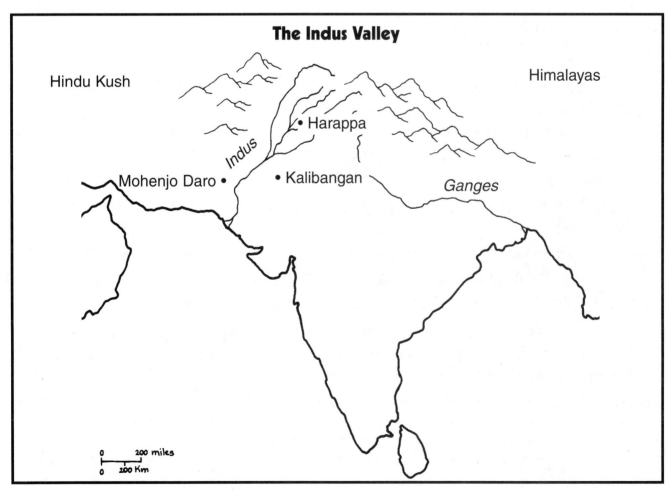

The Indus Valley

Hindu Kush

Himalayas

Indus

• Harappa

Mohenjo Daro •

• Kalibangan

Ganges

0   200 miles

0   200 Km

Background Information for the Teacher

Presented below and on page 8 are historical highlights of the origins of Hinduism. Share some of this information with students. Discuss the following questions: Who are the Aryans? Where did they settle? What are the Vedas? Who are the Brahmins? What is an ascetic? What is the importance of the ascetics in Hindu life?

The Aryan Invasion

Although there is evidence that the Indus Valley civilization may already have been struggling, its collapse began with the migration of the Aryan tribes around 3000 BCE. The Aryans, a powerful race, traveled through Europe and Asia, desending from the Hindu Kush and the Himalayas into the Indus Valley. They brought with them a very different belief system and way of life.

To begin with, the Aryans were not agricultural people. Rather than fertility symbols, they crafted beautiful bronze weaponry. Another major contrast was their religious focus. The Aryans were patriarchal, worshipping only male gods. Their central god was a "sky father," probably an influence of the Greek and Roman gods, Zeus and Jupiter. Their principal deities, such as Agni and Indra, were associated with the sun. Aryan priests composed verses to these gods which were recited during fire sacrifices.

The Aryans settled the lush Indus Valley and maintained their rituals. However, much of the Indus' religious culture remained alive in villages and was adopted by the Aryans. From this mixture of beliefs and practices, Hinduism was born.

The Vedas

With the Aryans arrived the bedrock of the Hindu thought system, the *Vedas*. Considered the world's oldest writings, these scriptures originated before the Aryans migrated to the Indus Valley, later evolving into four scriptures: the *Rig-Veda*, the *Yajur Veda*, the *Sama-Veda*, and the *Atharva-Veda*. The oldest and most popular of these is the *Rig-Veda*, a collection of hymns which may date back as early as 5000 BCE. It is important to note, however, that the historical sweep of Vedic writing reflects deep shifts in spiritual interest and ways of worship.

Interestingly, for centuries the Vedas were only transmitted orally, through memorization and recital. Eventually, however, they were transcribed into Sanskrit, the sacred Hindu language developed by the Aryans of the Indus Valley.

The *Rig-Veda* tells of thirty-three gods, all of whom are born of one creator, Brahman. Complementing Brahman are Vishnu and Shiva. These three gods form the Hindu trinity. The principal goddesses, Lakshmi, Sarasvati, and Kali are also part of the *Rig-Veda*. This variety of deities—many of whom take on different personalities and names—are very much alive in everyday Hindu life.

Background Information for the Teacher *(cont.)*

• • • • • • • • • • • • • • • The Ascetic • • • • • • • • • • • • • • •

By the 7th century BCE, Aryans, along with people of the Indus Valley, had migrated across India to the Ganges Valley, settling among the native population. Wherever they lived, the Aryans represented the elite of society, and the most elite were the *Brahmins*, or priests. These priests determined a class order, or caste system, which they included as a Vedic hymn. To this day, the caste system helps shape Hindu society.

Although the Brahmins were revered in the early Hindu periods, their role slowly began to be questioned. The Brahmins assumed spiritual authority, overseeing the writings of the Vedas and demanding complicated rituals. These rituals centered around the Brahmins and excluded those from lower classes. As disillusionment rose, a more individualized way of religious life was born, the life of the *ascetic*.

The ascetic was a person dedicated to a life of spiritual austerity and self-discipline. Untouched by the social system, ascetics often chose a hermitage in the forest or gathered with others to live lives of intense devotion and meditation. By example, these individuals inspired people away from dependence on priests, creating a revolution of spiritual thought and practice.

• • • • • • • • • • • • • *The Upanishads* • • • • • • • • • • • • •

From this revolution were born *The Upanishads*, authored by ascetics between 700 and 500 BCE. As the final part of the *Vedas, The Upanishads* contain almost exclusively dialogues of a *guru*, or spiritual master. In fact, *Upanishad* literally means "sitting beside" a guru. These texts differ from earlier Vedic writings in that they are intended to inspire and welcome anyone, regardless of status or caste. Although *The Upansihads*, like much of the Vedic writings, are difficult to absorb, what matters is the seeker's depth of sincerity and character.

It follows, then, that the fire rituals so common among Vedic priests were replaced by the deep internal searching of the ascetics. To the students of *The Upanishads*, the fire of understanding burns within. The fire rituals are metaphors for an inner revelation.

Central to Upanishadic belief is that of the *atman*, or higher self. The atman is a person's soul which must return to Brahman, the universal soul. Through meditation and self-sacrifice, an individual may come to realize fully that he is not separate from the universal soul, he is not a body or an isolated identity.

Note to the Teacher: The hymns and excerpts below and on pages 10 –11 are taken from important Hindu readings. Read and interpret these with students. As an extension, compare the passages to the teachings of other religious groups. What are some similarities and differences?

The Rig-Veda

The following passage is from the creation hymn, "The Unknown God, the Golden Embryo." The word *oblation* means "an offering to a god."

¹In the beginning the Golden Embryo arose. Once he was born, he was the one lord of creation. He held in place the earth and this sky. Who is the god whom we should worship with the oblation?

²He who gives life, who gives strength, whose command all the gods, his own, obey; his shadow is immortality—and death. Who is the god whom we should worship with the oblation?

³He who by his greatness became as one king of the world that breathes and blinks, who rules over his two-footed and four-footed creatures—who is the god whom we should worship with the oblation?

⁴He who through his power owns these snowy mountains, and the ocean together with the river Rasa, they say; who has the quarters of the sky as his two arms—who is the god whom we should worship with the oblation? (Rig-Veda 10.121 1, 2, 3, 4)

The Upanishads

The following excerpt is from "Isha," chapter two.

The Self is one. Unmoving, it moves swifter than thought. The senses do not overtake it, for always it goes before. Remaining still, it outstrips all that run. Without the Self, there is no life.

To the ignorant the Self appears to move—yet it moves not. From the ignorant it is far distant—yet it is near. It is within all, and it is without all.

He who sees all beings in the Self, and the Self in all beings, hates none.

To the illumined soul, the Self is all. For him who sees everywhere oneness, how can there be delusion or grief?

The Self is everywhere. Bright is he, bodiless, without scar of imperfection, without bone, without flesh, pure, untouched by evil. The Seer, the Thinker, the One who is above all, the Self-Existent—he it is that has established perfect order among objects and beings from beginningless time.

To darkness are they doomed who devote themselves only to live in the world, and to a greater darkness they who devote themselves only to meditation.

Life in the world alone leads to one result, meditation alone leads to another. So have we heard from the wise.

They who devote themselves both to life in the world and to meditation, by life in the world overcome death, and by meditation achieve immortality.

The Upanishads (cont.)

This next passage is from chapter nine, "Chandogya."

One day the boy Satyakama came to his mother and said: "Mother, I want to be a religious student. What is my family name?"

"My son," replied his mother, "I do not know who was your father. I am Jabala, and you are Satyakama. Call yourself Satyakama Jabala."

Thereupon the boy went to Guatama and asked to be accepted as a student. "Of what family are you, my lad?" inquired the sage.

Satyakama replied: "I asked my mother what my family name was, and she answered: 'I do not know. In my youth I was a servant and worked in many places. I do not know who was your father. I am Jabala, and you are Satyakama. Call yourself Satyakama Jabala!' I am therefore Satyakama Jabala, sir."

Then said the sage: "None but a true Brahmin would have spoken thus. Go and fetch fuel, for I will teach you. You have not swerved from the truth."

The Hindu Trinity

Hinduism is a polytheistic religion, meaning that its followers believe in more than one god. In fact, worshippers commonly devote themselves to one god, their personal deity. Household shrines feature pictures and statues of the chosen gods. Individuals may choose this god for its special attributes. For example, Ganesh, the god with the head of an elephant, is known for overcoming obstacles and bringing success.

Some of these gods appear in the famous Hindu epics, *The Ramayana* and *The Mahabarata*. These poems originated from the storytelling and parables of the Brahmins and ascetics. In present-day India, these stories are beloved and more popular than the *Vedas* and *Upanishads.* Accessible and entertaining, rich with heros and villains, they simultaneously provide moral and spiritual instruction.

The *Rig-Veda* introduced the foremost of the Hindu gods: Brahama, Vishnu, and Shiva. Although each of these deities possess special attributes, many Hindus believe they represent three properties of one god. Together they form the Hindu Trinity.

Brahma: The Creator

Brahma is considered the mystical creator, the supreme presence, or God. Many Hindus believe that all other gods originate from Brahma. To the right is a depiction of Brahma. His four faces stand for the four corners of the universe. He holds a sacrificial ladle, the four Vedas, a jar of holy water from the Ganges, and a necklace of prayer beads. Like all Hindu gods, he sits upon a lotus throne.

Vishnu: The Preserver

"Whenever the Sacred Law fails, and evil raises its head, I (Vishnu) take embodied birth. To guard the righteous, to root out sinners, and to establish Sacred Law, I am born from age to age." (Bhagavad Gita IV. 6–8)

Followers of Vishnu worship him as the preserver, greatest of the gods. His role is to maintain a balance between good and evil powers in the universe. In order to do this, Vishnu returns to Earth in different forms, both animal and human. Tradition holds that there are ten *avatars*, incarnations, linked to Vishnu. However, only Rama and Krishna remain the focus of worship among Hindus.

The Hindu Trinity

• • • • • • • • • • **Vishnu: The Preserver** *(cont.)* • • • • • • • • • •

Here are the ten incarnations of Vishnu and the task each performed:

1. **Matsya** (Fish): As a giant fish, Vishnu warned the world of a great flood, rescuing both a famous sage and the Vedas from the flood.

2. **Kurma** (Tortoise): After the flood, Vishnu, in the form of a huge tortoise, retrieved the gods' elixir of immortality, which was lost in the depths of the ocean.

3. **Varah** (Boar): After the demon Hiranyakasipu plunged the earth into the ocean, Vishnu, in the form of boar, hoisted the world above water.

4. **Narasimha** (Man-Lion): In order to destroy another demon, Vishnu became half-man, half-lion. This was because the demon, Hiranyakasipu, could be killed by neither animal nor man alone.

5. **Vamana** (Dwarf): When Vishnu first came as a human avatar, he did so to outwit the ruling demon-king, Bali. As a dwarf, he convinced Bali to give him as much land as he could cover in three steps. Immediately, Vishnu transformed himself into a giant, striding across the universe.

6. **Parashurama** (Rama with an axe): Vishnu returned as Rama with an axe to defeat the ruling warrior class and restore the Brahmins to power.

7. **Rama** (Prince): As prince of Ayodya, Rama is the hero of the epic poem, *The Ramayana.*

8. **Krishna** (Young hero and lover): Krishna is considered by many Hindus to be the most important avatar. Fleeing the King (his evil uncle), he was raised in a forest where he slayed many demons. Eventually, he killed his uncle and restored his kingdom. When he returned to the forest to battle demons, he was accidentally slain by the arrow of a follower. Krishna's charm and power are the subject of many stories in Hindu mythology.

9. **The Buddha:** Prince Siddhartha, the Buddha, was a great spiritual leader and founder of Buddhism.

10. **Kalki:** Yet to come, some Hindus believe Kalki will appear upon a white horse, yielding a flaming sword, at the end of time.

Shiva: The Destroyer

Shiva is worshipped as the destroyer or purifier. Like Vishnu, Shiva appears in many different forms throughout Hindu legends. However, the most widely known is that of Shiva Nataraja, the Lord of the Dance.

Shiva dances in a halo of fire, representing the cycle of birth and death. As he dances, he crushes the dwarf, the demon of ignorance. In his right hand, he keeps rhythm beating a drum, while in his left hand he holds the flame of destruction, purification, and renewal. His other hands are in a position of blessing or refuge. Around his arms and neck he wears deadly snakes. The snakes symbolize Shiva's power over evil forces, while its ability to shed its skin makes it a symbol of fertility, as well.

Use the information above to identify parts of Shiva.

Hindu Goddesses

The worship of the goddess in Hinduism has its roots in the Indus Valley civilization where the mother was revered as the renewer of life and as a symbol of fertility and strength. Like their male counterparts, each goddess possesses particular attributes, and worshippers adopt each for the personal qualities she brings.

Three of the principal goddesses are directly related to the gods of the Hindu Trinity: Saraswati, daughter of Brahma; Laxmi, wife of Vishnu; and Parvati, wife of Shiva. For many, Parvati, like Brahma, is the ultimate reality. She is the "great goddess" from whom all the goddesses are born. While an abundance of minor goddesses are featured in village shrines, Parvati is the central figure of goddess worship.

Parvati, like many Hindu deities, takes on many forms, some of which are very different in nature. Like her husband, Shiva, her role can either be forceful or self-sacrificing. One of her most popular and feared manifestations is that of Kali.

• • • • • • • • • • • Kali: Goddess of Strength • • • • • • • • • • •

This common depiction of Kali shows her wearing a necklace of human skulls while wielding a sword in one hand and the decapitated head of a giant dripping blood in the other. Her tongue hangs out and a third eye watches from her forehead. Because death cannot touch her, she is atop a corpse and resides in the cremation ground. As the ultimate symbol of death and pain, many Hindus revere Kali, believing that going beyond her will bring enlightenment.

Although Kali leaves behind her bloodshed and death, one legend tells of how she destroyed the terrible oppressor, Raktabija. Each time a drop of Raktabija's blood fell, multitudes of demons came to life. Kali rescued the world by slaying the tyrant and then draining his blood.

Extension

Research and describe each goddess' characteristics. Can you explain her posture, what she is holding, and why?

Laxmi: Goddess of Wealth and Good Fortune

_____

_____

_____

_____

_____

_____

_____

_____

_____

_____

Saraswati: Goddess of Knowledge and Art

_____

_____

_____

_____

_____

_____

_____

_____

_____

The Ramayana

The epic poem, *The Ramayana,* tells the story of the life of Rama, Prince of Ayodya. Rama is the seventh incarnation of Vishnu. This story, combined with *The Mahabharata,* represents the most celebrated tale in all of Hinduism. In fact, Hindus are often named after the colorful and profound characters of these epics. It is also common to see these deities worshiped in temples and during festivals.

Here is a brief retelling of the cycle of *Ramayana.*

THE CYCLE OF RAMAYANA

Our story begins in the city of Ayodya, capital of the land of Koshala, to the north of Benares, between the River Ganges and the Himalayas. Here lived Prince Rama and his younger half-brother, Lakshmana. Their father was King Dasharatha, ruler of Ayodya. Rama's mother was Kaushalya.

The brothers grew up happily, excelling in sports while mastering weaponry and horsemanship. But their real adventures began when the famous sage, Vishwamitra, asked for Rama's help in slaying a stronghold of *rakshasas,* forest demons. These demons plagued the forest-dwelling ascetics, ruining their fire sacrifices and defiling their altars. Although only teenagers, the boys accompanied the sage into the depths of the woodlands.

Soon, the brothers had won the hearts of their people by destroying demon after demon. Despite the evil spirits' powers of invisibility and great strength, Rama's arrows pierced them all, even the most terrible.

They returned with the sage to the city of Mithila, where the famous bow of Shiva was kept under the rule of King Janaka. The brothers were anxious to see the bow which no one—not king or sage—could string. Impressed by the brothers' heroism, King Janaka announced that if Rama could string Lord Shiva's bow, then the young prince would marry his daughter, Sita.

The Ramayana

THE CYCLE OF RAMAYANA (cont.)

Effortlessly, Rama lifted the mighty bow. And as he strung it, it broke in two with a thunderous sound.

Rama and Sita were married. Lakshmana and Sita's sister, Urmila, were also wed. When the couples returned to Ayodya, a festive welcome awaited them. There they lived happily for the next twelve years.

When the aging King Dasharatha had to name a successor, he chose Rama, his eldest son. Throughout the land the inhabitants celebrated, knowing that the prince would be a wise and brave leader. What they did not know, however, was that a crisis was about to befall Ayodya.

The trouble began when Kaikeyi, Dasharatha's third wife and mother of Bharata, heard the news that Rama was to be crowned. She was overjoyed, feeling as if Rama were her own son. However, her maid, Mantharama, had evil intentions. She worked relentlessly to convince Kaikeyi that Rama would have Bharata sentenced to death, even though Bharata was away in his grandfather's kingdom.

Now, years back, Kaikeyi had saved King Dasharatha's life. He had promised her any two things she wished, and she had saved these boons. Now she demanded that Bharata be made king and that Rama be exiled to the forest for fourteen years. The King, deeply distressed, tried to go back on his word, but Rama would not let him. Instead, he nobly agreed to Kaikeyi's terms, announcing that the most virtuous act was to keep his father's word.

THE CYCLE OF RAMAYANA (cont.)

Hearing this, Sita said she would join her husband. The dangers of the forest, she proclaimed, would be nothing compared to living without her husband. The loyalty of Lakshmana also compelled him to join his brother. So, without malice or regret, Rama clothed himself in the robe of an ascetic, blessed the throne for Bharata, and left for the forest with Sita and Lakshmana.

Deep into the forest traveled the three companions. But it was not long before they received a visitor, Bharata himself.

Having learned of Rama's exile, Bharata came to his brother in distress, asking Rama to return to Ayodya and assume his role as king. But again Rama stood firm: it was most important that their father's pledge to Kaikeyi remain unbroken. He would remain in exile. Bharata understood, proclaiming that he would rule on Rama's behalf. As a symbol of his elder brother's true authority, Bharata placed Rama's sandals on the throne.

After Bharata departed, Rama, Sita, and Lakshmana found a peaceful spot by a river. There they built a cottage. Living in harmony, the trio was esteemed by the sages of the forest. These ascetics were also thankful for the protection which Rama provided. Since his arrival, many Rakshasas were slain.

As news of Rama's might spread, the demons became angrier. In fury, they gathered an army of fourteen thousand and attacked, swearing to defeat their nemesis. At once, Rama ordered Lakshmana and Sita to take refuge in a nearby cave. Then, single-handedly, he defeated the massive demon army. However, the evil Akampana escaped Rama's arrow and flew in his carriage back to his ruler, Ravana. King of the Rakshasas, the demon Ravana had ten heads and twenty arms, standing giant and powerful.

THE CYCLE OF RAMAYANA (cont.)

Learning that Rama had slain his two brothers and thousands of other demons, Ravana swore vengeance. Aware of Rama's physical prowess, he plotted the kidnaping of Sita, for without his beloved wife, his source of love and devotion, the prince would surely die of a broken heart.

And so it was that Ravana, disguised as an ascetic, arrived at the forest home of the royal family. There he managed to lure Rama away in pursuit of a demon appearing as a beautiful deer. As the deer led Rama deeper into the woods, Sita worried and pleaded with Lakshmana to find her husband. It was then that Ravana appeared at the cottage.

Although she did not recognize Ravana, Sita sensed danger. At once, Ravana assumed his true form and abducted Sita. As they flew southward to the land of Lanka, he promised her riches and power if she would be his queen. Sita scoffed at his offer, warning that he would be destroyed by Rama.

Meanwhile, Rama and Lakshmana despaired. After discovering the deer's true identity, they returned to find Sita missing. Rama plunged into sorrow, vowing to destroy the world unless the gods restored Sita to his side. Just then, Jatayu, an aged vulture loyal to King Dasharatha, spoke to the brothers. Wounded and breathing his last breaths, the faithful bird had tried but failed to rescue Sita. Now the vulture told Rama that his wife was not dead, but kidnaped by Ravana. As the brothers buried Jatayu, they vowed to rescue Sita.

Knowing they would need help, Rama and Lakshmana sought out the well-known monkey, Hanuman. A strong bond grew between them, and soon Hanuman had gathered together an army of monkeys, promising to liberate Sita. Indeed, they already had some jewelry the Princess had dropped from Ravana's carriage. The legion searched and searched in all directions until they learned that Sita had been carried to the land of Lanka, in the southern ocean.

THE CYCLE OF RAMAYANA (cont.)

Although the monkeys were powerful animals, able to leap great distances, the vast stretch of ocean between the lands was disheartening. Only the mighty Hanuman, son of the wind god, possessed the divine energy to jump the great waters. They watched as Hanuman changed into a huge form and soared above the ocean at great speed.

When Hanuman finally reached Lanka, he leapt the city walls and began to search for Sita. He sneaked through the palace, but nowhere could he find the Princess. Finally, wandering the night, he found the captive Sita in a grove of trees. There he witnessed as Ravana tried in vain to lure Sita into marriage. But she would not budge, speaking only of her loyalty to Rama. At last, the demon king threatened to have her killed unless she consented.

When Sita was alone, Hanuman lowered himself from the trees. He gave her one of Rama's rings and offered to carry her home on his back. But Sita refused. She would be rescued, she declared, only by her husband who would destroy Ravana and restore her honor. Nothing short of this would she accept. Handing Hanuman a jewel, she bid the brave messenger return to Rama and deliver it to him.

And so Hanuman crossed the ocean once again to deliver the news of Sita's safety. Rama's heart swelled when he saw the jewel Sita had sent. And when he learned that she would be rescued by him alone, he felt heavenly pride.

Now, led by Rama and Lakshmana, the monkey troops gathered again on the shores of the sea. Suddenly, they saw a group of rakshasas flying toward them. Braced for attack, they were surprised to find that it was Ravana's younger brother, Vibhisan, come to seek refuge with them, for he would not take part in Ravana's evil scheme.

THE CYCLE OF RAMAYANA (cont.)

The newcomers were welcomed by the monkeys, who still faced a serious problem: how were they to cross the sea? They could not find a solution until Rama threatened to dry the waters himself if the ocean gods did not help. But as the enraged Prince lifted his bow, the Lord of the Ocean, Sagara, rose before him. Sagara instructed the army to build a bridge which his powers would support.

The monkeys worked furiously until the bridge was built and they crossed safely to Lanka. Ravana, witnessing their passage, gathered his soldiers for war, vowing to destroy Rama. Thus, the battle began.

All day, the demons and monkeys fought to a standstill. Slowly, though, the monkeys proved mightier. Seeing this, Ravana himself appeared on the battlefield, showering arrows upon his enemies. Rama acted at once, destroying Ravana's chariot, leaving the king defenseless before him. But in his honor Rama would not kill an unarmed enemy, and Ravana retreated, ashamed, to his palace.

It was not long, however, before the demon King returned fully armed for war. Now he raged and took deadly aim at Lakshmana. Ravana's arrow pierced the young man's heart. Rama, stricken with grief, lay by his dying brother's side. But a voice consoled him. The wise monkey, Sushena, knew of an herb from the distant mountain, Mahodaya. This herb would heal Lakshmana's wounds.

At once, Hanuman flew to the Himalayas. But when he reached the mountain, he did not know which herb to bring. So he gathered his strength and lifted the entire mountain back to Lanka! The monkeys watched in awe as Hanuman delivered the mountain. They found the correct herb and celebrated as Lakshmana was healed.

THE CYCLE OF RAMAYANA (cont.)

Just then, a war cry rent the air. Aboard a new chariot, Ravana attacked. Rama mounted his chariot and charged. The Prince of Ayodya and the king of the rakshasas battled fiercely. For a long time, the clanging of steel was all that was heard. Finally, Rama, invoking help from the gods, fired an arrow into Ravana's heart. The demon fell dead.

Lanka was captured and Sita set free. But as Rama approached her, he looked forlorn. He told Sita that they must part, that a husband cannot take back a wife who has lived in another man's house. But Sita had thought only of Rama during her captivity. How, she wondered tearfully, could he doubt her purity?

Boldly, she proclaimed that she would prove her purity. Sita ordered the monkeys to build a funeral pyre. When the wood was piled and set aflame, she walked three times around the pyre. Proudly, she bid farewell to the world and leapt into the fire.

But no harm came to Queen of Ayodya. Agni, the fire god, appeared before her and, leading her safely out of the flames, announced to Rama that she was indeed virtuous.

Rama, deeply moved, accepted his queen. Indeed, in truth he had never doubted her. If they were to rule the people of Ayodya, he knew, all suspicion must be removed.

Together, the royal pair returned to their kingdom, where they ruled for many years. Virtuous and wise, they brought order and happiness to the people of Ayodya and beyond.

The Ramayana

Comprehension Questions

On a separate sheet of paper, write your responses in full sentences. Feel free to review the story if you need.

1. Write the names of Rama's mother, father, and brother.

2. How did Rama first win his reputation?

3. How did Rama win Sita's hand in marriage?

4. Why does Kaikeyi have Rama exiled?

5. How does Bharata feel about Rama's exile? What does Rama say to him?

6. Knowing of the danger, why does Sita join her husband?

7. Describe Ravana's physical appearance.

8. Why does Ravana choose to kidnap Sita? How does he succeed?

9. Who tells Rama and Lakshmana about Sita's abduction?

10. Who is Hanuman? Why is he able to jump so far and change forms?

11. Why does Sita refuse to be rescued by Hanuman?

12. Why does Vibhisan seek refuge with Rama?

13. What happens when Rama lifts his bow to dry the ocean?

14. Why won't Rama kill Ravana when they first battle?

15. For what reason does Rama separate himself from Sita after her rescue?

16. How does Sita feel about this?

17. How does the story end?

The Ramayana

Critical Thinking

The Ramayana is an adventure rich in meaning. Although there is a great deal of action, this epic is meant to be instructive as well as entertaining. In the section below, write about each topic listed. Review the story and give detailed examples to support your findings.

1. Write about the role of virtue, or honor, in the story.

_____

_____

_____

_____

_____

_____

2. What role do the gods play in the story?

_____

_____

_____

_____

_____

_____

3. What role do animals play in the story?

_____

_____

_____

_____

_____

_____

The Ramayana

Essay

Although thousands of years old, *The Ramayana* involves many plot elements which remain popular to this day. For example, how many stories do you know where a princess is kidnapped and then rescued? Have you ever seen a movie starring a "demon king"? What about gods who intervene, or characters who change forms, or animals who speak and have special powers?

In the page below, compare a movie or book with a similar plot to *The Ramayana*. How are they similar? How are they different?

_____

_____

_____

_____

_____

_____

_____

_____

_____

_____

_____

_____

_____

_____

_____

_____

_____

_____

_____

Hindu Beliefs

In order to understand Hinduism, we must learn about a few basic beliefs which form the foundation of the religion. These beliefs are rooted in both *The Vedas* and *The Upanishads.* Besides defining a belief system, these ideas also carry into Hindu law and rites of passage.

Dharma

Dharma stands for the ultimate moral balance of all things. Dharma belongs to the universe and to the individual as well. So, just as there is a divine order of the natural and cosmic realms, there is the same order within a personal life. However, each one has the responsibility to balance his or her own dharma.

A Hindu's dharma is played out in all areas of life: religious, social, and familial. If a person makes a promise, the promise must be kept at all costs. Likewise, the faithful maintain their religious rituals while attending to their family's needs.

But what if an individual goes astray? This leads to the next major Hindu belief, karma.

Karma

The word *karma* has multiple meanings in Hinduism. In one sense it means duty. Hinduism believes that everyone should do his or her duty without expecting a favorable result. Karma also means destiny or fate.

Samsara

In the Western world, *samsara* is commonly known as reincarnation. Samsara represents the cycle of life, death, and rebirth in which a person carries his or her own karma. Each life cycle presents an opportunity for balance.

Therefore, an individual may experience effects from past lives, although the circumstances may be totally different. In fact, many Hindus believe that a person's worldly status depends upon actions in a past life. Likewise, good thoughts and actions can liberate a person. Some Hindus believe that certain people meet in more than one life in order to achieve karmic balance. Thus, every relationship and situation becomes meaningful.

What happens, then, when a person becomes purified? Is reincarnation an eternal process, or is there another realm? The answer lies in moksha.

Moksha

Like heaven for the Christian, Hindus strive to reach *moksha*, or a state of changeless bliss. Moksha is achieved by living a life of religious devotion and moral integrity without any interest in worldly things. However, it may be many lifetimes within the wheel of life before moksha is achieved. The ultimate reward is release from samsara and union with God.

Hindu Beliefs

Personal Response

1. Do you have a sense of dharma in your own life? Explain.

   _____

   _____

   _____

   _____

   _____

2. Does our society have a sense of dharma? Explain your answer.

   _____

   _____

   _____

   _____

   _____

3. How is the story, "The Boy Who Cried Wolf," an example of karma? Can you think of other examples, even in your own life?

   _____

   _____

   _____

   _____

   _____

4. Describe a book or movie which contains the idea of samsara.

   _____

   _____

   _____

   _____

   _____

Places of Pilgrimage

Religious pilgrimage plays an important role in Hinduism. There are many holy sites in India, each dedicated to a certain god, a group of gods, or a famous happening. At these centers of worship, the devotee is energized by history, by the meeting of the spiritual and the earthly. Although there is no definite route to follow, every practicing Hindu is encouraged to complete a pilgrimage to all four religious sites in a lifetime.

Within India, these principle places of pilgrimage rest on the four compass points. Hindus visit these sacred spots in a popular all-country route. A four-site pilgrimage normally lasts ten weeks.

Look on the map on page 30. Beginning at Rameshravaram at the southern tip of India, the pilgrims proceed in clockwise order until they encircle the country. If you recall from *The Ramayana*, this is where Rama and Hanuman's troops built a bridge to Lanka in order to rescue Sita. The principal deities worshipped here are Vishnu and Shiva.

Next, the devout journey to Dwarkadheesh in western India where Vishnu is deified. From there, they travel to Badrinath in the far north. There, high in the Himalayas, rests another shrine to Lord Vishnu where for centuries Hindus have worshipped. The faithful are then likely to visit the source of the sacred River Ganges at Gangotri.

From the thin air of Badrinath, the travellers follow the Ganges southward to the populated city of Calcutta, and then they proceed onward to Puri. Thousands of Hindus gather here annually in July for a great temple festival worshipping Krishna as "Lord of the Universe." Joyous crowds follow as a forty-six foot (13.8 m) image of Lord Krishna aboard a massive chariot is paraded through the streets.

Completing this pilgrimage is a difficult task requiring self-discipline and spiritual austerity. Hindus, therefore, place great emphasis on such journeys, whether they include all of India or not. Since Hindus regard life as a pilgrimage toward enlightenment, each holy destination fosters the religious connectedness needed to advance spiritually.

Other Pilgrimage Sites

Besides the four locations mentioned above, India is rich with pilgrimage sites. One such place is Haridwar, meaning "Lord's Gate." On the banks of the Ganges, Hindus commit the ashes of the dead into the holy water.

Below is a list of other important places of pilgrimage. Do some research to find out the significance of each area. What took place there? Who is the principal god? What is the form of worship? Respond below and on the back of this paper.

1. Vrindavan _____

2. Ayodya _____

3. Ujjain _____

4. Benares _____

5. Kanchipuram _____

6. Gaya _____

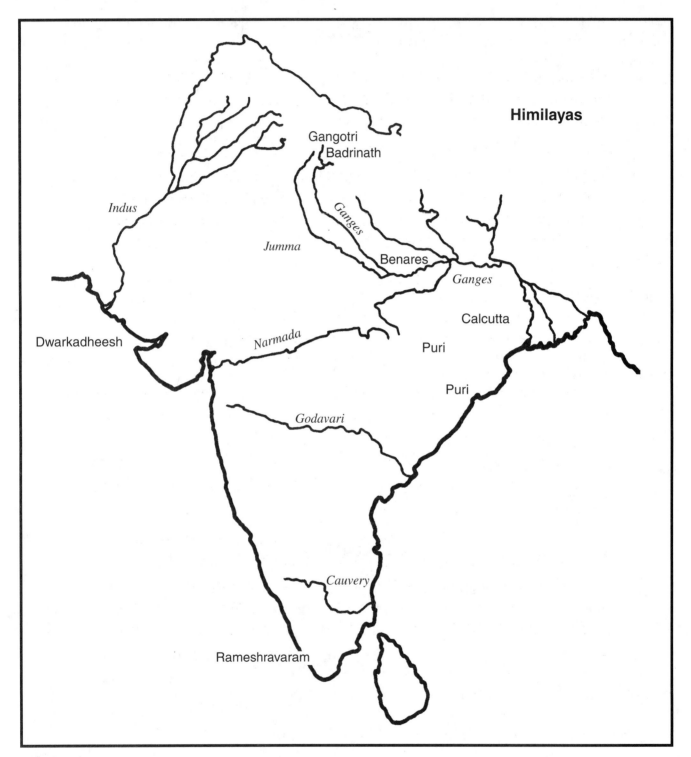

Extension

Throughout history, people have been making pilgrimages. These journeys are not always tied to a religion, although many are. If you were to go on a pilgrimage, where would you go? Why? What would be required of you? Write an essay describing your personal journey. Remember to include lots of details.

Water

The people of the Indus Valley considered water sacred. To Hindus, water is both literally and symbolically a source of life, renewal, and hope.

The River Ganges, born in the Himalayas and nourishing the holy city of Varanasi, is the most venerated river in all of India. Countless people visit its banks every year, washing themselves or committing the ashes of a loved one into its waters. In either case, there is the belief that contact with sacred rivers helps balance a person's karma.

There are many stories surrounding the origin of the Ganges. One of the most famous myths tells the story of Ganga, a goddess with the power to purify anything that touched her.

The story tells of the royal family of King Sagara, and his queens, Keshini and Sumati. Sumati alone has 60,000 sons, all regal and enthusiastic. So when the sacred sacrificial horse is stolen from the palace, the princes eagerly quest for its return. They search the entire surface of the earth without luck. Finally, in their haste, they dig into the netherworld. This disturbs the planet's balance, causing a tremendous earthquake.

Unaware of the harm they have done, the boys discover the sacrificial horse in the presence of the sage, Kapila. They accuse Kapila of stealing the horse, and they prepare to attack him. But the powerful sage, enraged by their accusation, utters one syllable and engulfs the 60,000 in flames, reducing them to ashes.

Water *(cont.)*

Later, Amsuman, the nephew of the brothers, meets with Kapila. The sage explains that there is only one way the thoughtless princes can escape suffering in hell forever: Ganga, in all her purity, must descend from heaven and touch the ashes of the cursed uncles.

But neither Amsuman nor his son, Dilipa, is able to bring Ganga to Earth. But when Dilipa's son, Bhagiratha, refuses to take the throne until Ganga descends, Lord Brahma is impressed. The god offers Bhagiratha a boon, and the prince asks that Ganga descend. But Brahma cannot grant the boon. The earth, he explains, would be destroyed by the force of Ganga's current. Only Shiva could withstand it.

So Bhagiratha performs penances until Shiva agrees to receive Ganga's mighty force. But when the goddess tries to sweep Shiva into the netherworld, she is imprisoned in the matted locks of his hair. Again, Bhagiratha worships Shiva, begging for pity. Shiva, moved by the prince's sincerity, releases Ganga, who has been purified by contact with Shiva's hair. Soon, many people rush to Ganga to be cleansed.

But on their way to the netherworld, Ganga disturbs the meditations of sage Jahnu, who consumes her in one swallow. Devastated, Bhagiratha again must beg for release. Finally, Jahnu frees the captured goddess, who is even more pure after her contact with the sage.

At last, Bhagiratha and Ganga flow over the earth, the ocean, and into the netherworld. The sons of Sagara are redeemed, and Brahma promises that Ganga will continue to flow, offering purification to all the faithful.

The Hindu Class System

Varna

The Hindu class system, *varna*, is rooted in the traditions of the Aryan people. The Brahmins, or high priests, determined a class order using Vedic hymns as testimony. Take, for example, this excerpt from the famous verse, "The Hymn of Man":

> [11] When they divided the Man, into how many parts did they apportion him? What do they call his mouth, his two arms and thighs and feet?

> [12] His mouth became the Brahmin; his arms were made into the Warrior, his thighs the People, and from his feet the Servants were born." (*Rig-Veda*, 10.90 11, 12)

Using the human body as a metaphor, this hymn divides society into four distinct classes, or castes, based on occupation. The mouth is the Brahmin, priest. The arms are the Shatriyas, warriors and rulers. The thighs are the Vaishyas, skilled workers and farmers. The feet are the Shudras, servants.

Although people are expected to marry within their own caste, they have not always done so. Because of inter-caste marriages, *jatis*, subdivisions of castes, were established. If a couple within the three higher strata are mixed, their children represent a new caste below the Vaishyas but above the Shudras. But if an individual from one of the three upper classes should wed a Shudra or a non-Hindu, the descendants become *Pariahs*, untouchables. Lowest on the social scale, the untouchables are considered outcasts of society.

The system of jatis is complex and varied, depending greatly on region and history. Once a new jati is established, its members are again encouraged to marry within its ranks.

It is important to remember that rank in the caste system is linked to dharma. By performing familial and social duties honestly, a Hindu strives to be born into a higher caste in his or her next incarnation. But the opposite is also true. If a member of an upper class is without virtue, he or she may be born a Shudra or Pariah.

Presently, the constitution of India does not recognize the ancient caste system, prohibiting its social distinctions. Many Hindus believe the varna is unjust, separating the wealthy from the poor while providing no opportunity for betterment. Still, many of the system's jatis still exist, especially in India's countless villages.

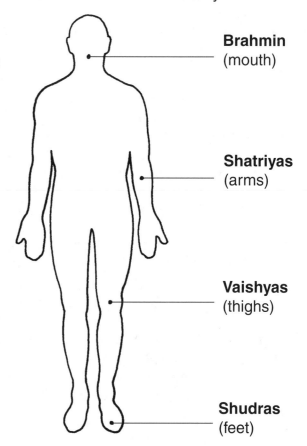

Brahmin (mouth)

Shatriyas (arms)

Vaishyas (thighs)

Shudras (feet)

Rites of Passage

• • • • • • • • • • • • • • • • Birth • • • • • • • • • • • • • • •

Even before a baby is born, Hindus perform rituals and recite prayers to protect the fetus from illness or harmful spirits. The mother eats only healthy foods to ensure the newborn's well-being.

In some families, the father performs a ceremony immediately after the birth. He dips a gold pen into a jar of honey and writes the sacred Sankrit symbol, Om or Aum, onto the infant's tongue. (See illustration.) The symbol, which stands for truth, is written in hope that the child will be honest and speak only the truth, which is sweet as honey.

After a little more than a week, the baby's name is formally given. Usually the name of a favorite god or goddess is chosen and whispered into the child's ear.

Within the first few years of her life, a Hindu girl has an ear-piercing ceremony. Both boys and girls have their hair cut, symbolic of renewal and the shedding of wrongdoing in past lives.

The Ceremony of the Sacred Thread

The Ceremony of the Sacred Thread is an ancient rite of passage into adolescence reserved for male members of the three upper castes, the Brahmins, Shatriyas, and Vaishyas. Like the Jewish bar mitzvah, it represents a rebirth or initiation into the religious community.

Traditionally, this rite of passage served to introduce the devotee into religious life. In the presence of a guru, or holy teacher, the young man shaves his head and dons a saffron robe. Taking up a simple walking stick, he renounces all material possessions and then receives the sacred thread. The unadorned thread is symbolic of the interconnectedness of all things. It consists of seven strands, each of which represents a different virtue or quality. They are as

| Power of speech | Intelligence | Steadfastness | Good reputation |
| Memory | Forgiveness | Prosperity | |

The boy promises to embody these qualities, and for the rest of his life he wears the sacred thread as a symbol of his coming-of-age.

The ceremony concludes with a fire sacrifice, the most common form of ritual in Hinduism. In early times, the initiate would follow his teacher into a faraway dwelling to study scriptures and to lead a life of spiritual practice and austerity. Afterwards, he would reenter society, marry, and raise a family. Nowadays, only young men seeking to become priests or ascetics live with a guru.

Rites of Passage

• • • • • • • • • • • • • • • • Marriage • • • • • • • • • • • • • • •

Most Hindu marriages are arranged by the parents, although the children must also be happy with their chosen partner. Hindus almost always marry within the same caste, although in modern times there are increasing exceptions.

A wedding is one of the most colorful and important ceremonies in all of Hinduism. Although customs vary greatly in different regions, marriages are always joyous, momentous occasions, rich with decorations and food. In fact, some Hindu weddings last as long as three days!

The ceremony centers around a sacred fire, a manifestation of the god, Agni. Family and friends surround the couple as a priest chants Sanskrit verses. Next, he leads the bride and groom around the flames which burn in a brick firepit. Bells are sounded, and many offerings are made to the fire, including clarified butter, grains, and flowers. Each time the couple completes their circuit, the bride stands on one of the bricks. This act affirms her strength and loyalty.

Finally, the bride and groom take seven steps around the flames. These steps are the most significant action in a Hindu wedding. Now the couple is bonded for life, their union sanctified.

• • • • • • • • • • • • • • • • Death • • • • • • • • • • • • • • • • •

Since ancient times, cremation, or the burning of corpses, has been a Hindu custom. Like the marriage ceremony, the rite of passage into death centers around the sacred fire.

The funeral begins when the body is wrapped in cloth and carried away on a stretcher. As family and friends leave their village for the cremation grounds, they recite prayers to the chosen deity of the deceased. Traditionally, the eldest son lights the wood of the funeral pyre with a flame lit in a nearby temple. Prayers and offerings are made in the belief that the deceased is going through a process of rebirth, cleansed by the fire into new life. The ritual also protects the relatives from evil spirits.

The ceremony concludes when the ashes are thrown into a river. Many Hindus want their remains to be left in the River Ganges, believing that its waters will help purify their souls.

Response
Choose one of the previous four rites of passage. On a separate piece of paper write your response to the customs of the rite.

Like a church, synagogue, and mosque, the Hindu *mandir*, or temple, is a holy place of gathering and worship. Although mandirs vary in grandeur, they all share some specific features.

To begin with, each temple is dedicated to a particular god, although representations of other gods are allowed. In fact, *mandir* actually means "dwelling." At the heart of the temple rests a shrine to the chosen deity. These shrines contain an image—usually a statue or painting—of the god. Each morning the priest adorns the shrine, surrounding the image with fresh flowers, fruit, incense, candles, lamps, and other decorations.

Hindus believe that although an image cannot contain God, deeper understanding can be achieved by meditating on a representation of Krishna, Vishnu, Brahma, or other deities. It is in this spirit that Hindus perform *puja*, daily worship. Temple pujas are performed at dawn, noon, dusk, and midnight. Participants take an active role in their worship, beginning with *darshan*, which simply means "to focus upon a deity." Next, the devotee makes a food offering. The priest blesses the *prasad*, or food, which is then consumed by the worshipper. It is also common for the priest to burn some of the gift and smear the consecrated ashes on the giver's forehead. Finally, some temples have room for followers to circle the shrine in a clockwise motion, another popular form of worship.

Traditionally, the outside walls of a mandir are decorated with sculptured representations of an array of mythic and worldly happenings. In fact, some older temples are literally carved out of rocks and caves. Some of these sculptures are magnificent, intricate works of art. Other temples are simple, unadorned buildings. Some rise into spires, or towers, symbolizing the meeting of the celestial and earthly. The entrance, usually facing east, welcomes the guest into a pillared hallway, an assembly hall, or both. These lead to the shrine room, the heart of the structure. Many temples also contain bathing tanks where devotees cleanse themselves.

Unlike the members of many other religions, Hindus may maintain their spiritual devotion without visiting their house of worship. As you will see, many worship their chosen deity at their family shrine. Still, the mandir serves an essential role in the spiritual life of a Hindu. It is a place where the world is left behind for awhile, a place of ritual, devotion, and cleansing.

Extension

On the next page, study the sketch of the essential parts of a mandir. Follow up by finding some photos of a Hindu temple and locating these features.

Mandir means "abiding place" or "dwelling." It is the home of the god worshipped there. The main services at a mandir are at sunrise and sunset.

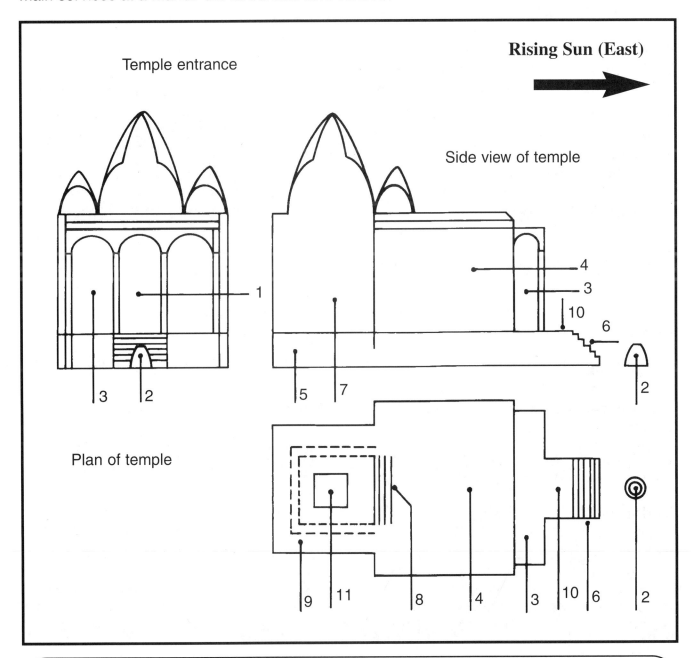

Temple entrance

Rising Sun (East)

Side view of temple

Plan of temple

PARTS OF THE MANDIR

1 Temple entrance	5 Basement	9 Processional passage
2 Stone Image	6 Steps	10 Porch
3 Pillared hallway	7 Shrine room	11 Images
4 Hallway	8 Steps to the shrine	

Almost all Hindus keep a shrine in their home, regardless of their caste or economic status. These shrines, dedicated to a particular god, vary in size. Some families can afford to leave aside an entire room while others can devote only a corner of the bedroom. In either case, the sacred space, like the shrine of a temple, is tended to religiously. Here, family members worship collectively or individually.

Notice the common features of the family shrine on the right. On a table or shelf rests a photograph of the chosen god. The fragrance of fresh flowers and fruit mixes with incense and perfumes in the air. A bell, which is rung for prayer, stands nearby. Other symbols, gods, and gurus may also appear in the shrine.

Daily Duties

Beside daily worship, most Hindus attend to four other religious duties. Here is a list explaining all five daily duties:

1. **Worshipping God:** Hindus must devote part of their day to worship. This ensures spiritual contact.

2. **Reciting scripture:** By reciting from a sacred text, the faithful learn the lessons of worldly and religious life.

3. **Honoring parents and elders:** Hindus are very loyal family members. Parents and elders are honored for their wisdom and self-sacrifice.

4. **Helping the poor:** Even the less fortunate try to obey this commandment. Guests, in particular, are given special attention in a Hindu home.

5. **Feeding animals:** Because Hindus consider all life a sacred part of one god, animals are respected and cared for.

Make Your Own Shrine

Set aside part of your room for a personal shrine. The shrine can focus on your religious tradition or it can just be a place to put special things. For example, you may want to decorate your area with a favorite souvenir or a letter from a dear friend. Take a picture of your shrine and bring it to class to share.

Be sure to look after the shrine area. Keep it decorated and clean.

Om or Aum

The symbol *Om*, or *Aum*, is the principal symbol of Hinduism. It is both a visual and an oral representation of Bramha, or God. This mark has another name, *Pravana*, which means "that by which God is effectively praised," and "that which is ever new." Hindus repeat the word Om in order to transcend their individual thoughts and merge with God.

Actually, Om is comprised of three independent letters, "a," "u," and "m." The letter "a" represents beginning, "u" means progress and "m" stands for dissolution. Thus, Om reflects the power responsible for the creation, development, and destruction of the universe.

This symbol is the most widely used in all Indian religions, appearing in both Buddhism and Sikhism.

Sri Yantra

The geometrical pattern, *Sri Yantra*, is commonly used as a visual focal point for meditation. It originated with the Sakti cult, the votaries or worshippers of the Divine Mother. The design itself represents the form of the goddess. The Sri Yantra consists of nine triangles which intersect to form forty-three triangles in all. Three concentric circles surround the triangles. The shape is framed by a square.

This symbol represents spiritual evolution. The triangles stand for the many aspects of God, which, when focused upon, merge into one. When this occurs, consciousness of unity appears in the circles. Finally, the entire symbol is seen as a single unit mirroring the Absolute, or God.

Objects and Symbols

The Swastika

The swastika is an ancient symbol of auspiciousness, good fortune, and protection. The root, "swasti," literally means "auspicious." Besides being used as a symbol for Vishnu, it also represents the eternal wheel of life which rotates upon an unchanging center, God. In India, it is not uncommon to find swastikas marked on buildings and animals. Some Hindus believe it protects them from evil spirits and natural disasters.

It is important to understand that the Hindu swastika predates the swastika of Nazi Germany by centuries. In fact, the Nazi symbol is actually drawn in the reverse of the Hindu one.

The Lotus

The lotus bud, which is born in water and unfolds itself into a beautiful flower, symbolizes the birth of the universe, manifesting itself in all its glory. It is also a symbol of the sun, which rises in the navel of Vishnu. The lotus is the seat of Brahma as well. In fact, many deities are depicted sitting atop the sacred lotus flower.

The Cow

For ages, the cow has been held sacred by Hindus. The cow is the offspring of the celestial cow, which was created by Lord Krishna from his own body. Another Hindu myth says the cow was born of the churning of the ocean. Also, the earth often approaches God in the form of a cow.

For many Hindus, the cow is a sacred animal, providing milk and butter. Both these products are used in rituals of atonement.

Floor Paintings

If you were to visit India, you would notice colorful floor paintings decorating the entrance to many homes. These designs, which are not permanent, are made with chalk or rice flour. The patterns can be simple or complex. In either case, they keep alive a spirit of blessing and care for the home.

The Sri Yantra (at the right) is one challenging design. Hindus use this design as a focus for meditation.

Make a Floor Painting

Use colored chalk to design your own floor painting. Look through a book that contains Indian art and, with permission, copy a design for your school or home.

Use colored beans, grains, and cardboard (or construction paper) for a textured appearance.

Directions

1. Choose a pattern you like and sketch it onto the cardboard (or construction paper).

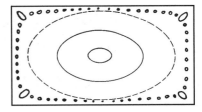

2. Plan your colors by writing them on the areas where they belong.

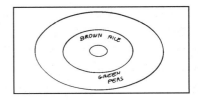

3. Fill the sections with glue and cover with beans and grains. Let the painting dry thoroughly.

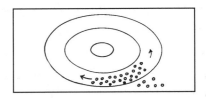

Observances

• • • • • • • • • • • • • • • • Divali • • • • • • • • • • • • • • •

Divali, which means "a row of lights," celebrates the Hindu New Year. Because Hindus follow a lunar calendar, this holiday can fall in either October or November. Also known as the "Festival of Lights," people decorate their streets and doorways with small clay lamps called *divas* (or *idpas*). All this is done in anticipation of the coming of Lakshmi, the goddess of prosperity and good fortune. Colored lights and fireworks add to the festive atmosphere, for only if Lakshmi is greeted with light will she offer her blessings of wealth and abundance.

Divali lasts for five days. The faithful carefully clean their homes and businesses, while decorating their floors with colorful floor paintings made of rice flour. Everyone wears his or her finest clothes and jewelry and, in the spirit of generosity, offers sweets and gifts to friends and neighbors.

For some Hindus, Divali also commemorates the homecoming of Rama and Sita after their long years in exile. When the royal couple returned, their city was alight with lamps.

Extension

Before a friend's birthday, or to welcome somebody home, make several small ceramic pots, leaving enough room in each for a candle. Surprise the person by lining his or her house with these handmade lights!

• • • • • • • • • • • • • • • • Holi • • • • • • • • • • • • • • • •

Holi is the Hindu spring festival, celebrating the equinox and the coming of Lord Krishna, who played with the colors of life. In northern India, Holi is also the time to gather the winter harvest.

A favorite among children, the holiday begins in the evening when bonfires are lit. These fires are meant to empower the sun as it moves into the warmer and longer hours of spring. All night the faithful sing and dance and pray around the bonfires. When dawn arrives, the fires are extinguished with water.

Now, instead of fire, water becomes the center of the festival. People throw water, colored with special dyes, at each other in a playful spirit. These antics last for three days, during which people spend leisure time together, eating special holiday foods and sweets.

Extension

With your teacher's permission, celebrate the spring equinox (March 20) with water games. Do some research to find out how you can safely color the water so that it does not stain.

Like the Jewish and Islamic calendars, Hindus follow a lunar year. This means that each month begins with the appearance of the new moon, causing festivals and holidays to appear at a different date each year. The fortnight, or first two weeks, of the waxing moon is called *Shukla Paksha*. The fortnight of the waning moon is called *Krishna Paksha*.

Here are the months of the Hindu calendar along with their Gregorian equivalent. Below, you will also find a list of major festivals and the months in which they fall.

HINDU MONTHS

Magha (Jan./Feb.)	**Phalguna** (Feb./March)	**Chaitra** (March/April)	**Vaiskha** (April/May)
Jyestha (May/June)	**Ashadha** (June/July)	**Sravana** (July/August)	**Bhadrapada** (August/Sept.)
Asvina (Sept./Oct.)	**Karttika** (Oct./Nov.)	**Margasirsha** (Nov./Dec.)	**Pausa** (Dec./Jan.)

SOME SIGNIFICANT FESTIVALS AND HOLIDAYS

Magha: *Maker Sankranti Lohri*, winter solstice festival

Phalguna: dedication to Saraswati, goddess of poetry and wisdom

Chaitra: *Holi*, spring festival

Vaisakha: *Ram Navami*, Rama's birthday celebration

Ashadha: *Ratha Yatra*, celebration of Krishna

Bhadrapada: *Raksha Bandhan*, holiday celebrating siblings; *Janamashtami*, celebration of Krishna's birth

Karttika: new year festival; *Divali*, festival of lights

Extension

Research a holiday from this list and write a short essay on its history and festivities.

Hindu Crossword Puzzle

Across

2. Hinduism originated in the _____ Valley.
4. The most sacred river in India
6. "What goes around comes around."
9. An _____ lives a life of solitude and meditation.
10. Considered the world's oldest writings
12. The goddess of strength
15. Hindu heaven
17. Daughter of Brahma, she is the goddess of knowledge and art.
19. Pariahs, or _____ , are at the bottom of the social scale.
20. Shiva wears these around his arms and neck.

Down

1. The priests, or elite of society
3. The sacred text which opened the doors of spirituality to all castes
5. The destroyer
7. In the Western world, samsara means _____ .
8. The goddess of wealth and good fortune
11. Stands for the moral balance of all things
13. Brahma is known as the _____ .
14. Poem that tells the story of the life of Rama
16. The preserver, he has ten incarnations
18. The _____ system divides people into different social levels.

Quiz and Review

Part One: For questions one through ten, fill in the spaces with the correct answers.

1. When a child is born, Hindus use _____ to write the sacred symbol _____ on the newborn's tongue.

2. The rite of passage into adolescence for male Brahmins is called the ceremony of the _____ .

3. A Hindu wedding is complete when the bride and groom take _____ steps around the flames.

4. _____ is the customary rite of passage into death.

5. Many Hindu rituals center around _____ , the god of fire.

6. _____ or the Festival of Lights, celebrates the New Year. This holiday is in honor of the goddess _____ .

7. Holi celebrates the _____ equinox and welcomes Lord _____.

8. A Hindu temple is called a _____ .

9. An image of the chosen deity is kept in a _____ .

10. The geometric Sri Yantra is used for _____ . It originated with worshippers of the _____ .

Quiz and Review

Part Two: Answer the following prompts in the spaces below.

1. Explain the three main principles of the Hindu belief system: dharma, karma, and samsara.

   _____

   _____

   _____

   _____

2. Discuss and describe the Hindu caste system. Why does it exist?

   _____

   _____

   _____

   _____

3. Explain the role and meaning of fire in Hindu weddings and funerals.

   _____

   _____

   _____

   _____

4. How do Hindus worship? Describe what you might see if you were to visit a Hindu temple.

   _____

   _____

   _____

5. List and describe the five daily duties of a Hindu.

   _____

   _____

   _____

   _____

If you have ever read about something that happened long ago, then you are probably familiar with the abbreviations BC or BCE and AD or CE. Buddha was born in 563 BCE. Muhammad died in 632 CE. Both BC and BCE represent the years before the birth of Jesus. CE and AD mean the years after the birth of Jesus. The abbreviations stand for the following:

BC = Before Christ
AD = Anno Domini (in the year of our Lord)

BCE = Before the Common Era
CE = Common Era

In this book, only BCE and CE are used. This is because BC and AD relate all dates to the birth of Jesus. Referring to Jesus as Christ or using dates that are based on the birth of Jesus are part of the Christian religion.

You have probably also read of events happening, for example, in the 5th century or even in the 5th century BCE. A century is 100 years. If people lived in the 1st century, they lived in the first 100 years CE, or in the first 100 years after the birth of Jesus. So, if we say something happened in the 19th century, we mean it happened during the years 1801–1900 CE. The same rule applies to the centuries BCE, only we count backwards from the birth of Jesus. For example, Buddha was born in 563 BCE, which would mean he was born in the 6th century BCE.

Here are some practice questions. You will need to use the sample time line and your math skills to find the answers.

2000 BCE	1500 BCE	1000 BCE	500 BCE	0	500 CE	1000 CE	1500 CE	2000 CE

1. Who is older, someone born in 1760 BCE or someone born in 1450 BCE?

   _____

2. How many years difference is there between 250 CE and 250 BCE?

   _____

3. How many years difference is there between 1524 CE and 1436 BCE?

   _____

4. You visit a cemetery. One of the tombstones reads: "Born in the 15th century, died in the 16th." Make up possible dates that this person may have been born and died.

   _____

5. In what century are you living now?

   _____

Answer Key

Page 6

1. artifacts and relics found through archaeological digs
2. a. a bank tank at Mohanjo-Daro: ritual bathing important to Hindus
   b. terra-cotta figurines: represent fertility, strength, rebirth, and continuity, central to Hindu faith
   c. bulls: represent virility, sacred to the Hindus
3. agricultural people, dependent on water, water still sacred to Hindus

Page 11

Answers will vary.

Page 16

Answers will vary.

Page 24

1. King Dasharatha, Queen Kaushalya, Lakshmana
2. by destroying demons
3. by stringing Lord Shiva's bow
4. She was tricked into believing Rama would have her son sentenced to death.
5. Bharata is very upset. Rama tells him to rule the kingdom.
6. She could not live without him.
7. Ravana, the giant, has ten heads and twenty arms.
8. He knew Rama would die of a broken heart. He disguises himself.
9. Jatayu, the old vulture, tells Rama.
10. Hanuman is a monkey and he is son of the wind god.
11. She would be rescued only by her husband so her humor would be restored.
12. He did not want to be involved with Ravana's evil.
13. The Lord of the Ocean appeared with instructions.
14. Rama would not kill an unarmed enemy.
15. A husband cannot take back a wife who has lived with another man.
16. She is hurt.
17. The royal couple returns to Ayodya as rulers.

Page 25

Answers will vary.

Page 26

Answers will vary.

Page 28

Answers will vary.

Page 44

Across

2. Indus
4. Ganges
6. karma
9. ascetic
10. Vedas
12. Kali
15. moksha
17. Saraswati
19. untouchables
20. snakes

Down

1. Brahmin
3. Upanishads
5. Shiva
7. reincarnation
8. Laxmi
11. dharma
13. creator
14. Ramayana
16. Vishnu
18. caste

Page 45-46

Part One

1. honey; Aum or Om
2. Sacred Thread
3. seven
4. Cremation
5. Agni
6. Divali; Laxmi
7. spring; Krishna
8. mandir
9. shrine
10. meditation; Divine Mother

Part Two

1. karma-cause and effect of one's actions
   samsara—reincarnation
2. caste system based on Aryan tradition; born into a caste because of personal merit; endeavor to do better for next lifetime
3. fire means renewal, cleansing; husband and wife circle it, used for cremation
4. in temple would see offerings to shrine, circling shrine, taking of prasad, prostration, meditation, chanting, prayer to dieties
5. (1) worship God (2) recite scripture (3) honor parents and elders (4) help poor (5) feed animals

Page 47

1. 1760 BCE
2. 500 years
3. 2960 years
4. Answers will vary. One possibility is 1450-1550.
5. It is the 21st century.